Thirty-One Fantastic Recipes

CHEESECAKE

by Lou Seibert Pappas

Illustrations by Reynold Ruffins

CHRONICLE BOOKS

SAN FRANCISCO

Acknowledgments   With many thanks to a delightful food friend and critic, Cathie Colson, and to a coterie of devoted tasters from Stanford Singles.

Text copyright © 1993 by Lou Seibert Pappas
Illustrations copyright © 1993 by Reynold Ruffins

Edited by Meesha Halm
Designed by Laura Lovett
Printed in Hong Kong

Library of Congress Cataloguing-in-Publication Data

Pappas, Lou Seibert.
    Cheesecakes/by Lou Seibert Pappas: illustrations by Reynold Ruffins.
        72 p.   165 x 165 cm.
        ISBN 0-8118-0322-8
        1. Cheesecake (Cookery)   I. Title.
    TX773.P27   1993   92-47463
    641.8'653–dc20   CIP

Distributed in Canada by
Raincoast Books, 8680 Cambie Street, Vancouver, B.C. V6P 6M9

10 9 8 7 6 5 4 3 2

Chronicle Books 275 Fifth Street, San Francisco, CA 94103

Contents

Recipe Chapters

Introduction

Sensuous, seductive, sublime: that's cheesecake! It's a mouth-filling morsel of creamy richness that explodes with flavor.

Once I discovered this sumptuous dessert, it became addictive. When I was reared in the Northwest on *The Joy of Cooking* in the thirties and forties, cheesecake was often bypassed among our daily dessert repertoire. The commercial Hobart mixer in the sunny, yellow-tiled kitchen was always whirring out sweets—honeymoon special lemon pie, strawberry schaum torte, wild blackberry tarts, Boston cream pie, and whipped cream chocolate roll—yet a pineapple Bavarian cheese pie was the closest temptation to the true product.

My first encounter with real cheesecake was on an East Coast summer sojourn as a college freshman. Embarking by train on the Shasta Daylight, I stopped in San Francisco, New Orleans, Washington, D.C., New York, and Boston, dining at notable restaurants en route.

A yellowed scrapbook with menus from the Tadich Grill, Antoine's, Arnaud's, Durgin Park, the Toll House Restaurant, and the Stork Club notes, "the cheesecake was marvelous at the Big Apple," and only there was it offered. With one biteful of thick, dense New York cheesecake, I was smitten with a passion for more.

In the fifties and sixties as a Bay Area food editor at the West Coast magazine *Sunset*, I created cheesecakes in countless styles and flavors. Since then, on more than three dozen trips abroad, cheesecake slipped into my dining format. A strawberry-topped version was a love early on, with the sun-sweet refreshing berries countering the paradisal filling. Tangy raspberry purée was always a favored embellishment, often arriving with a feathered swirl of cream. French roast coffee beans whizzed to espresso fineness produced another winning flavor. Kahlua, Amaretto, and rum lent their aromatic lift, and a praline topping was enthralling to my palate. Chocolate fiends indulged in bittersweet or white chocolate versions underscored with a chocolate crust.

Lately experiments with streamlining the fat content have revealed some luscious light styles, with no apologies in order. Yogurt cheese plays a key role in several versions and the wide availability of worldly fruits with exotic overtones has prompted new flavors. A cheese glacé sampled in Provence has inspired a blissfully light framboise cheesecake.

As tastes have expanded to global fare, savory cheesecakes with an ethnic flair have become a fascination, as they make great party pleasers or entrées. The filo-wrapped pies with a shattering wafer-thin crust and melting cheese filling are tantalizing appetizers and are a carryover of my fondness for Greek cuisine. A pesto-striped torte and a smoked salmon pie are other delights. As Southwest fare arrived in the spotlight, a Santa Fe-style cheesecake became apropos.

Today the great variety of cheeses prompts flavors sweet and savory, both light and classic, with nuts, chocolate, fruits, and liqueurs to please all. Cheesecake making is joyfully easy and almost foolproof. The potential creations are many-fold, with irresistible tastes to enchant every devotee.

Cheesecake through the Ages

Since time began, this esteemed sweet has played a role in culinary lore. The ancient Greeks are credited with being the originators of cheesecake. It was made to fortify athletes during the first Olympic Games on the Isle of Delos in 776 B.C. Later it became the custom for brides to bake little cheesecakes for the friends of their groom, thus commencing the wedding cake tradition. Pastries were fashioned with goat's or ewe's milk cheese, then dried for a long-lasting food for soldiers and sailors.

The origin of cheese itself is considered unknown. Perhaps it was discovered by shepherds in the Indus Valley or Mesopotamia 6,000 to 8,000 years ago when they carried milk in a pouch made from a sheep's or goat's stomach. As the milk came in contact with the rennet in the stomach lining, it would coagulate into cheese. Cheese molds for draining the curds have been found in ruins dating to 2,000 B.C., indicating that cheese was a common food then.

With the Roman conquest of Greece, cheesemaking spread. The ancient Romans built special kitchens just for making cheese and cooking it, and cheesecakes were a treat for citizens of modest means as well as the rich. As Julius Caesar conquered the Continent and the Roman Empire spread throughout Europe, the Romans discovered that cheese was already a dietary staple there. Food customs intertwined and new combinations evolved. In Europe, the Church and monks began producing cheese dishes and cheesecakes for nourishment and income.

The cross-cultural blending of Middle European traditions and English ones spawned a great variety of cheesecakes. In the Russian Orthodox Church, cheesecakes became an Easter tradition, and they also played a role in Mediterranean holiday celebrations.

Samuel Pepys, in his diary dated August 11, 1667 noted, "some of the best cheesecakes ever eaten in my life." The *Art of Cookery* by Mrs. Hannah Glasse, published in 1747, listed saffron and lemon cheesecakes, among others. Immigrants to America brought the knowledge of cheese cookery with them. In trying to duplicate the then popular Neufchâtel cheese of France, American dairymen in 1872 achieved cream cheese, an unripened cheese even richer than Neufchâtel. It took James L. Kraft to develop a method of pasteurizing cheeses in 1912.

The popularity of cheesecake was naturally sparked by the

advent of the silver-wrapped packages of Philadelphia cream cheese. *The Settlement Cookbook* of 1915 contains a number of cheese pies and kuchens, baked in pastry or a raised sweet dough. With the accessibility of freezers, frozen cheesecake has become a favored supermarket item, and the passion for cheesecake has prompted shops specializing in it alone to open throughout the country. While innovative restaurant chefs have sparked a new interest in cheesecake, prize cheesecakes can be whipped up with ease in the home kitchen.

Ingredients

Naturally cheese is the most essential ingredient in any cheesecake. The types of cheeses vary widely. Cream cheese, Neufchâtel or low-fat cream cheese, cottage cheese, and ricotta are commonly used. In savory cheesecakes, chèvre, Brie, Camembert, creamy Havarti, feta, Jarlsberg, and blue cheeses are other possibilities. Homemade yogurt cheese can also be used.

The butterfat content and the moisture vary among cheeses. Cream cheese contains at least 33 percent butterfat and 50 percent water content, or per ounce, 10 grams of fat and 100 calories. Neufchâtel drops to 23 percent butterfat with about 7 grams of fat per ounce and 70 calories. The water content rises to 60 percent and the texture is a little lighter and softer than cream cheese. Do not confuse this with the French Neufchâtel, which is similar to a Camembert and a totally different product. If you are really counting calories and fat, Neufchâtel or low-fat cream cheese can sometimes be substituted, but expect a slightly moister cheesecake.

Some purists prefer using natural cream cheese made without the gum additives, yet other cooks vie for the flavor of regular cream cheese. It all depends on individual preference.

Cottage cheese comes in various styles with butterfat ranging from ½ percent to 4 percent. Large curd cottage cheese yields a less grainy product than small curd cottage cheese, once it is blended, so many recipes specify it. It may be blended in a blender or food processor or pushed through a sieve two or three times to smooth it out.

Ricotta is available made from whole milk or low-fat milk. The grainy texture becomes more pronounced in the low-fat products.

Light cheeses include Jarlsberg at 80 calories and 4 grams of fat per ounce and Chavrie, a fresh goat cheese with a sharp, creamy delicious flavor and 50 calories and 4 grams of fat per ounce.

Heavy cream and sour cream or low-fat sour cream are other ingredients. Note that sweet heavy cream is about 40 percent butterfat and 50 calories per tablespoon with 6 grams of fat. Sour cream contains 20 percent butterfat and about 30 calories per tablespoon or 3 grams of fat. Low-fat or light sour cream is approximately 15 calories per tablespoon and 1½ grams of fat. Plain low-fat yogurt is approximately 9 calories per tablespoon and ¼ gram of fat. If the lower fat products are used in a recipe, expect a lighter, more custardy texture.

When butter is specified, unsalted butter is preferable to regular butter because it contains less salt and moisture.

Eggs add body and texture to

cheesecake and compensate for the high moisture content in cheese and cream, as they can absorb water. Recipes are based on large-sized eggs.

Granulated sugar is used most frequently in cheesecake for sweetening. Brown sugar or honey gives a darker color and more intense flavor.

All-purpose flour and cornstarch are used to thicken the batter and stabilize the moisture content.

Freshly grated lemon and orange zest are preferable to dried peels as the fresh peels contain aromatic oils. Nuts—almonds, hazelnuts, pistachios, pecans, walnuts, macadamia nuts, and pine nuts—add another taste and texture dimension. The flavor of nuts is often enhanced with oven toasting in a 325 degree oven. If hazelnuts are toasted, remove the papery skins, as they can take on a slightly burned essence during toasting.

A top quality chocolate supplies optimum flavor. Avoid artificial or chocolate-flavored products. Freshly roasted coffee beans finely ground to an espresso powder lend a rich coffee flavor to cheesecake.

Vanilla extract, cognac, and such liqueurs as Amaretto, Frangelico, Kahlua, Framboise, Kirsch, Cointreau, Triple Sec, or Grand Marnier are other enhancers.

Techniques and Tips

Cheesecakes are relatively easy and foolproof to make. A few pointers help avoid the pitfalls. s.

Allow the cream cheese to warm to room temperature before mixing. It will then blend smoothly and incorporate easily with the other ingredients. When mixing the cream cheese with the sugar and eggs, make sure that they are completely blended and smooth before adding the sour cream or heavy cream. Once the batter is thinned out, any cheese lumps present become difficult to smooth out. A mixer or a food processor can be used to blend the batter.

If possible, let eggs reach room temperature before using. This way the egg whites will beat to a larger volume. Beat egg whites just until they form soft upright peaks; do not overbeat. Use a clean bowl and electric beater with a wire whip or a hand-held wire whisk. Any contact with fat or detergent will prevent the whites from beating to optimum volume. Blenders or food processors are not suitable for beating egg whites or whipping cream

as they will not properly incorporate the usual volume of air.

Fold in the egg whites or whipped cream gently with a whisk or spatula using a scooping motion coming from the bottom of the bowl. Once incorporated, pour the batter into the pan and bake immediately.

In baking, cheesecakes require a moderately low baking temperature. The best test for doneness is appearance. The sides should be barely raised and starting to take on a golden color and the center may still be soft, but it will firm up as the cake cools. Let cheesecakes cool gently, preferably in the oven for 1 hour with the oven door open slightly. This is particularly important with a soufflé-style cake in order to avoid a cracked surface. If it is not possible to let the cake cool in the oven, remove it from the oven and place it on a rack to cool.

To avoid cracking during cooling, run a knife or spatula along the edge of the pan so that the cake can pull away freely as it contracts.

Refrigerate most cheesecakes for at least 4 to 6 hours before serving to enhance the flavors and let them firm up. To do this, leave the cake in the pan and cover the top of the pan with foil or plastic wrap to avoid odors and prevent it from drying out.

Most of the following recipes call for the standard 9-inch springform pan. A 7-inch springform pan is also used for some of the smaller cakes, ideal for 4 to 6 servings.

Leftover cakes can be refrigerated for two to three days. For longer storage, freezing is suitable for the rich, dense cakes. The lighter, more custardy or soufflé-like cakes do not freeze as well. It is not recommended to freeze cakes made with cottage cheese or Neufchâtel cream cheese.

If you are making several cheesecakes for a party and have just one pan for baking, one solution is to wrap a 9-inch cardboard disk in foil and use it on top of the metal bottom. This way the cake can be easily removed on its cardboard base and another one baked right away.

In cutting the cake, the filling often sticks to the blade, so it is smart to wipe the knife with a damp towel between each cutting.

Some chefs prefer to bake cheesecake in a waterbath, sealing the pan in foil before placing it in the oven in a pan containing hot water. The result is an evenly creamy cake throughout without a dry edge. These recipes avoid that extra step as the slightly firm edge with its tinge of golden brown is desirable.

Equipment

Mixer—useful for creaming cream cheese to a smooth consistency, blending the major ingredients, whipping cream, or beating egg whites.

Food processor—handy for whipping cream cheese, blending cottage cheese to a smooth consistency, making graham cracker crumbs, chopping nuts, or grating chocolate.

Blender—useful for making cracker crumbs or grinding nuts.

Coffee grinder—desirable for grinding coffee beans for flavoring.

Sieve—appropriate for straining cottage cheese or making yogurt cheese.

Springform pans—available in diameters of 7, 8, 9, and 10 inches. The sides are held tightly closed by a clip which can be released to allow the walls of the mold to spring into an expanded position. The wall or sides can then be lifted up and away.

Other useful tools include rubber spatulas, measuring spoons, and a double boiler.

Classic and Chocolate

Cheesecakes

Chocolate Decadence Cheesecake 22

Praline Crunch Cheesecake 24

Cheesecake Supreme 25

White Chocolate Cheesecake 26

New York Cheesecake 29

Chocolate Walnut Cheesecake 30

Chocolate Marble Cheesecake 31

Chocolate Decadence Cheesecake

This satiny chocolate cheesecake bakes without a crust and is embellished with Kahlua whipped cream and chocolate curls. Bittersweet chocolate is preferable for its extra intensity.

Place chocolate in the top of a double boiler and melt over hot water. Or place in a microwavable bowl and microwave on medium for 2 to 3 minutes or until melted. Let cool. In a food processor or mixer, place the cheese and sugar and process or mix until blended. Add eggs and vanilla and mix until smooth. Blend in chocolate and

8 ounces bittersweet or semisweet chocolate

1 pound natural or regular cream cheese

¾ cup sugar

4 eggs

1 teaspoon vanilla extract

1½ cups sour cream

Whipped Cream Topping:

½ cup heavy cream

1 tablespoon sugar

¼ cup sour cream

*1 tablespoon Kahlua
or other coffee-flavored
liqueur*

*Chocolate curls for
garnish*

sour cream. Pour into a greased 9-inch springform pan. Bake in the middle of a preheated 300 degree oven for 35 minutes or until the outer edge is set and the inner center is still glossy. Turn off the oven, leave the door ajar, and let cool in the oven for 1 hour longer. Chill.

Prepare Whipped Cream Topping: In a small bowl, whip cream until stiff peaks form and beat in sugar, sour cream, and liqueur. Spoon in a ring around the top of the cheesecake and sprinkle with chocolate curls. To serve, remove pan sides and cut into wedges.

Makes 12 to 14 servings.

TIP: Chocolate curls are easily made by shaving a small bar of bittersweet or semisweet chocolate with a vegetable peeler. For larger curls, melt 2 ounces of the chocolate and spread it in a thin layer on the back of a baking sheet. Let cool until set. Then holding a metal spatula perpendicular to the pan, pull it across the chocolate, forming large curls.

Praline Crunch Cheesecake

The topping on this caramel soufflé cheesecake is reminiscent of the delicious sugary praline patties indigenous to New Orleans.

In a large bowl of a mixer, beat cheese until creamy, then beat in brown sugar, cornstarch, and vanilla. Add egg yolks and beat until smooth. Mix in sour cream. In another bowl, whip egg whites until soft upright peaks form and fold into the cheese mixture. Pour into an ungreased 9-inch springform pan. Bake in the middle of a preheated 325 degree oven for 40 minutes or until set.

Prepare Praline Topping shortly before cake is finished baking. In a small skillet, melt butter over medium heat, add nuts and heat until lightly toasted, shaking the pan. Stir in brown sugar and cream. Bring quickly to the boil and cook, stirring, for 1 minute. Immediately drizzle over hot cheesecake. Turn off the oven, leave the oven door ajar, and let cool in the oven for 1 hour longer. Chill. To serve, remove pan sides and cut into wedges.

Makes 12 to 14 servings.

1 pound regular or natural cream cheese

1 cup firmly packed brown sugar

1 tablespoon cornstarch

1 teaspoon vanilla extract

4 eggs, separated

¾ cup sour cream

Praline Topping:

2 tablespoons butter

½ cup chopped pecans or sliced almonds

½ cup firmly packed brown sugar

1½ tablespoons heavy cream

Cheesecake Supreme

This lemon-scented cheesecake is a decades-old classic recipe. The egg white meringue and whipped cream lighten its style. Don't worry if it cracks slightly on top—it is unimportant.

In the food processor or mixer, process or mix the cheese until creamy and mix in half of the sugar, the egg yolks, vanilla, lemon zest, and flour, beating until smooth. In a bowl, whip egg whites until soft peaks form and beat in remaining sugar. In another bowl, whip cream until it mounds gently. Fold part of the meringue into the cheese mixture to lighten it, then fold the cheese mixture into the remaining meringue. Fold in whipped cream. Pour into a greased 9-inch springform pan. Bake in the middle of a preheated 300 degree oven for 1 hour or until a light golden brown and set. Turn off oven heat and let cake stand in the oven 1 hour longer. Chill. To serve, remove pan sides and cut into wedges.

Makes 10 to 12 servings.

1¼ pounds natural or regular cream cheese

⅞ cup sugar

4 eggs, separated

1½ teaspoons vanilla extract

2 teaspoons grated lemon zest

⅓ cup all-purpose flour

1 cup heavy cream

White Chocolate Cheesecake

A hint of white chocolate subtly imbues this snowy cheesecake and a dusting of cocoa emphasizes its chocolate status. It makes a spectacular presention on a berry sauce, garnished with whole berries.

Place chocolate in the top of a double boiler and heat over hot water until it melts. Stir to blend and let cool to room temperature. Place in a food processor or mixer the cheese and sugar, and process or mix until smooth. Mix in eggs, vanilla, and sour cream. Stir in melted chocolate. Pour into a greased 9-inch springform pan. Bake in the middle of a preheated 325 degree oven for 25 minutes or until just barely set. Turn off the oven, leave the door ajar, and let cool in the oven for 1 hour longer. Chill. Just before serving, dust cocoa through a sieve making a ring around the cheesecake.

Prepare Raspberry Sauce: Reserve ½ cup raspberries for garnish. In a food processor or blender, purée remaining berries and push through a sieve. Stir in sugar to taste. To serve, spoon Raspberry Sauce on dessert plates. Remove pan sides of cheesecake and cut into wedges. Place on Raspberry Sauce and garnish with berries.

Makes 10 servings.

6 ounces white chocolate chips

1 pound natural or regular cream cheese

¾ cup sugar

3 eggs

1½ teaspoons vanilla extract

¾ cup sour cream

2 tablespoons unsweetened cocoa

Raspberry Sauce: (optional)

2½ cups raspberries

Sugar to taste

TIP: It is important to have the cheesecake ingredients and the melted chocolate close to the same temperature when they are combined so they blend together smoothly. If the temperatures are at extremes, the chocolate can seize or clump together.

New York Cheesecake

This big, ultra-rich cheesecake is sublime as is, or top it with strawberries for a tantalizing treat.

Prepare Zweiback Crust: In a bowl, mix together the crumbs, butter, and sugar and press into the bottom and partly up the sides of a 9 or 10-inch springform pan. Bake in a preheated 325 degree oven for 8 minutes or until lightly browned. Let cool.

In the food processor or mixer, place the cheese and sugar and process or mix until blended. Add eggs and blend until smooth. Mix in flour, lemon zest, and cream. Pour into the crust-lined pan. Bake in a preheated 400 degree oven for 10 minutes; reduce temperature to 250 degrees and continue baking 35 to 40 minutes longer or until just barely set. Turn off the oven, leave the door ajar, and let cool in the oven for 1 hour longer. Chill. To serve, remove pan sides and cut into wedges.

Makes 16 servings.

STRAWBERRY CHEESECAKE VARIATION: Prepare New York Cheesecake as directed above. Wash and hull 2 cups medium-sized strawberries. Arrange, points up, on the cheesecake. In a microwavable bowl, heat 2 tablespoons currant jelly or seedless raspberry jelly in a microwave on high for 40 seconds or until melted. Or heat in a small saucepan until melted. Drizzle over the berries.

Zweiback Crust:

1¼ cups crushed zweiback crumbs

3 tablespoons melted butter

1 tablespoon sugar

2 pounds natural or regular cream cheese

1⅓ cups sugar

4 eggs

2 tablespoons all-purpose flour

2 teaspoons grated lemon zest

⅓ cup heavy cream

Chocolate Walnut Cheesecake

A tender bittersweet chocolate crust encases this ultra-rich cheesecake that flaunts a trio of flavors.

Prepare Chocolate Crust: In a mixing bowl place butter, sugar, cocoa, and flour and mix until crumbly. Pat into the bottom and partly up the sides of a 9-inch spring-form pan. Bake in a preheated 325 degree oven for 20 minutes. Let cool.

Place walnuts in a baking dish and bake in a preheated 325 degree oven for 8 minutes or until lightly toasted. Let cool and chop finely. With the back of a spoon, mash orange zest with 1 tablespoon sugar to release the oils. In a food processor or mixer, process or mix cheese until creamy, then add remaining sugar, eggs, and cream, mixing until smooth. Stir in the chocolate shreds and nuts. Pour into the crust-lined pan. Bake in the middle of a preheated 325 degree oven for 30 minutes or until just barely set. Turn off the oven, leave the oven door ajar, and let cool in the oven for 1 hour longer. Chill. To serve, remove pan sides and cut into wedges.

Make 10 servings.

NOTE: If desired, garnish with milk chocolate curls.

Chocolate Crust:

6 tablespoons butter, softened

3 tablespoons sugar

¼ cup unsweetened cocoa

¾ cup all-purpose flour

½ cup walnuts

Zest of 1 orange, finely chopped

¾ cup sugar

1 pound natural or regular cream cheese

3 eggs

½ cup heavy cream

3 ounces milk chocolate, finely shredded

Chocolate Marble Cheesecake

Bittersweet chocolate swirls through this golden cheesecake, lacing it with a candy-like confection.

Prepare Graham Cracker Crust: Mix together in a bowl the cracker crumbs, butter, and sugar. Pat into the bottom and partly up the sides of a greased 9-inch springform pan. Bake in a preheated 325 degree oven for 8 minutes. Let cool.

Place chocolate in the top of a double boiler and melt over hot water. Or place in a microwavable bowl and microwave on medium for 2 minutes or until melted. Let cool. Place cheese and sugar in a food processor or mixer, and process or beat until blended. Add eggs, sour cream, and vanilla and mix until smooth. Spoon out ¼ cup of the cheese mixture and stir it into the chocolate. Pour remaining filling into the baked crust. Spoon chocolate mixture over the light filling in distinct blobs. With a fork or spatula, gently swirl chocolate into the light filling to marble it. Bake in the middle of a preheated 325 degree oven for 25 minutes or until just barely set. Turn off the oven, leave the door ajar, and let cool in the oven for 1 hour longer. Chill. To serve, remove pan sides and cut into wedges.

Makes 10 servings.

Graham Cracker Crust:

1 cup crushed graham cracker crumbs

3 tablespoons melted butter

2 tablespoons sugar

3 ounces bittersweet or semisweet chocolate

1 pound natural or regular cream cheese

¾ cup sugar

3 eggs

½ cup sour cream

1 teaspoon vanilla extract

Fruit, Nut, and Liqueur

Cheesecakes

Liqueur Cheesecake Mold in a Fruit Wreath 34

Amaretto Cheesecake 35

*Kahlua-Espresso Cheesecake with Chocolate
Coffee Beans* 37

Hazelnut Cheesecake 38

Grand Marnier Cheesecake 39

Paskha 40

Kiwi Fruit Macadamia Nut Cheesecake 42

Gingered Sweet Potato Cheesecake 43

Golden Apple Cheesecake 44

Liqueur Cheesecake Mold in a Fruit Wreath

This luscious cheese mold is an interlacing of the French coeur à la crême *and the Italian mascarpone cheese. It makes a chic presentation with a wreath of fresh berries or other fruits.*

In a mixing bowl, beat together cheese and sugar and beat in cream, lemon zest, and liqueur. Line a 1 pint mold (such as a heart, flower, or pyramid) with a double layer of cheesecloth, allowing the ends to overlap the mold. Spoon in the cheese mixture, smooth top, and arrange the remaining cheesecloth over the top. Cover and chill.

Prepare Raspberry Strawberry Sauce: In a food processor or blender, purée raspberries and push through a sieve, discarding seeds. Purée strawberries and add. Stir in framboise, if desired, and add sugar to taste. Pour into a serving pitcher.

To serve, unmold cheese onto a platter and ring with berries or other fruit. Cut cheese mold into wedges, spoon onto dessert plates, garnish with fruit, and drizzle with Raspberry Strawberry Sauce.

Makes 8 servings.

1 pound natural cream cheese

¼ cup unsifted powdered sugar

⅓ cup heavy cream

1½ teaspoons grated lemon zest

3 tablespoons Cointreau or other orange-flavored liqueur

Raspberry Strawberry Sauce:

1½ cups raspberries

1 cup strawberries

1 tablespoon framboise (optional)

Sugar to taste

Fresh fruits: strawberries, raspberries, and blackberries or halved apricots, sliced nectarines or peaches, and seedless grapes for garnish

Amaretto Cheesecake

Almond liqueur and nuts too enhance this creamy cheesecake.

Spread nuts in a baking pan and bake in a preheated 325 degree oven for 8 minutes or until lightly toasted. Let cool and finely chop. Place in a food processor or mixer the cheese and sugar, and process or beat until smooth. Mix in eggs, vanilla, Amaretto, and sour cream. Reserve 2 tablespoons of nuts and stir in remaining nuts. Pour into a greased 9-inch springform pan. Sprinkle reserved nuts over the top. Bake in the middle of a preheated 325 degree oven for 25 minutes or until just barely set. Turn off the oven, leave the door ajar, and let cool in the oven for 1 hour longer. Chill. To serve, remove pan sides and cut into wedges.

Makes 10 servings.

½ cup whole almonds

1 pound natural, regular, or Neufchâtel cream cheese

¾ cup sugar

3 eggs

1 teaspoon vanilla extract

2 tablespoons Amaretto

¾ cup sour cream

Kahlua-Espresso Cheesecake with Chocolate Coffee Beans

Grind dark roast coffee beans ultra fine to flavor this seductive cheesecake. For a crunchy candy garnish, coat some beans in chocolate to ring the top.

Prepare Chocolate Crust, if desired, and let cool.

Using a coffee grinder, grind beans to a fine powder. Place in a food processor or mixer the cheese and sugar, and process or beat until smooth. Mix in eggs, coffee powder, vanilla, Kahlua, and sour cream. Pour into the crust-lined pan or a greased 9-inch springform pan. Bake in the middle of a preheated 325 degree oven for 25 minutes or until just barely set. Turn off the oven, leave the door ajar, and let cool in the oven for 1 hour longer. Chill.

Prepare Chocolate Coffee Beans: Place chocolate in a small bowl and heat over hot water until it melts. With a small spatula or fork, dip each bean in the chocolate and turn to coat. Place on foil and let cool until set.

To serve, garnish top of cheesecake with Chocolate Coffee Beans, remove pan sides of cheesecake, and cut into wedges.

Makes 10 servings.

Chocolate Crust: page 30 (optional)

¼ cup dark French roast coffee beans

1 pound natural or regular cream cheese

¾ cup sugar

3 eggs

1 teaspoon vanilla extract

3 tablespoons Kahlua

¾ cup sour cream

Chocolate Coffee Beans:

½ ounce bittersweet chocolate or semisweet chocolate chips

20 dark roast coffee beans

Hazelnut Cheesecake

Frangelico, the alluring hazelnut liqueur, and toasted hazelnuts lend a captivating overtone to this harmonious cheesecake. Fresh fruit in season—raspberries, apricots, white peaches, or nectarines—makes an ideal accompaniment.

Prepare Shortbread Pastry: Place flour, butter, and sugar in a food processor or mixer, and process or mix until coarse crumbs form. Pat into the bottom and partly up the sides of a 9-inch springform pan. Bake in a preheated 350 degree oven for 12 minutes or until lightly browned. Let cool.

Place nuts in a baking dish and bake in a preheated 325 degree oven for 10 minutes or until lightly toasted. Let cool for 2 minutes, then rub nuts between two paper towels, using your hands, to remove skins. Finely chop nuts. Place in a food processor or blender the cottage cheese, cream cheese, and liqueur, and process or blend until smooth. Blend in sugar, eggs, and cornstarch. Turn into a bowl, and stir in cream and nuts. Pour into the pastry-lined pan. Bake in the middle of a preheated 325 degree oven for 1 hour or until set. Turn off the oven, leave the oven door ajar, and let cool in the oven for 1 hour longer. Chill. To serve, remove pan sides and cut into wedges.

Makes 12 servings.

Shortbread Pastry:

1 cup all-purpose flour

½ cup butter

2 tablespoons powdered sugar

¾ cup hazelnuts

1½ pints (3 cups) large curd cottage cheese

8 ounces natural or regular cream cheese

¼ cup Frangelico or Amaretto

1 cup sugar

4 eggs

2 tablespoons cornstarch

1 cup heavy cream

Grand Marnier Cheesecake

Whipped cream elevates this orange-spirited cheesecake, giving it a soufflé-like quality. It's a natural to partner with seasonal strawberries, raspberries, nectarines, or peaches.

Prepare Cookie Crust: In a small bowl mix together cookie crumbs and butter and press into the bottom of a 9-inch springform pan. Bake in a preheated 325 degree oven for 8 minutes or until lightly browned. Let cool.

Mash orange zest with 1 tablespoon of the sugar to bring out the oils. In a food processor or blender, process the cottage cheese and cream cheese until smooth. Blend in remaining sugar, eggs, liqueur, orange zest, and cornstarch. In a mixing bowl, whip cream until soft peaks form and fold into the cheese mixture. Pour into the crust-lined pan. Bake in the middle of a preheated 325 degree oven for 50 minutes or until set. Turn off the oven, leave the oven door ajar, and let cool in the oven 1 hour longer. Chill. To serve, remove pan sides and cut into wedges.

Makes 10 to 12 servings.

Cookie Crust:

1¼ cups crushed shortbread, vanilla wafer, or butter cookies

3 tablespoons butter, melted

1 tablespoon grated orange zest

¾ cup sugar

1 pint large curd cottage cheese

8 ounces natural or regular cream cheese

3 eggs

¼ cup Grand Marnier or other orange liqueur or orange juice

3 tablespoons cornstarch

¾ cup heavy cream

Paskha

Candied orange peel, golden raisins, and slivered almonds jewel this traditional Russian Easter dessert. It also makes a splendid complement to year-round fresh fruits, or spread it on toasted brioche and top it with raspberry preserves.

Place raisins in a microwavable dish, add cognac, and microwave on high for 20 seconds to plump raisins. Or bake in a preheated 325 degree oven for 10 minutes or until hot through. Let cool. In the top of a double boiler whisk egg yolks until light, add sugar, and whisk until pale in color. Stir in cream. Place over simmering water, and stirring, cook until custard coats a spoon. Remove from heat, stir in vanilla and lemon zest, and let cool to room temperature. In a food processor or mixer, place butter and cheese, and process or beat until blended. Add custard and mix until smooth. Stir in the plumped raisins and diced candied orange peel. Arrange a double layer of cheesecloth in a conical cheese strainer or a clean 5-inch flowerpot or a charlotte mold. Spoon in the cheese mixture; gather up the ends of the cheesecloth and twist. Place strainer or mold in a pan to catch the liquid and cover top of strainer or mold with plastic wrap. Place a close-fitting plate and a weight, such as a 2 pound can, on top. Refrigerate 2 days, twisting the ends of the cheesecloth several times to squeeze out the liquid.

To serve, unmold on a serving plate and peel off cheesecloth. Garnish with nuts, candied orange peel, and raisins, or fresh fruit.

Makes 10 to 12 servings.

⅓ cup golden raisins

1 tablespoon cognac or brandy

4 egg yolks

⅔ cup sugar

½ cup heavy cream

1 teaspoon vanilla extract

2 teaspoons grated lemon zest

¼ cup butter, at room temperature

2 pounds (1 quart) ricotta cheese

⅓ cup finely diced candied orange peel

⅓ cup each toasted slivered almonds, slivered candied orange peel, and golden raisins, or 2 cups fresh fruit: strawberries, halved apricots, sliced nectarines, or pears, for garnish

Kiwi Fruit Macadamia Nut Cheesecake

Crispy sweet macadamia nuts underlie this cake-like cheesecake, sealed with cartwheels of emerald green kiwi fruit. This is also excellent topped with 1½ cups strawberries or blueberries and drizzled with melted currant jelly.

Prepare Macadamia Nut Crust: Butter the bottom and sides of a 9-inch springform pan. In a food processor or blender, process the crackers until fine, add macadamia nuts and process until finely chopped. Pat into the bottom of the springform pan.

In a food processor, blend cream cheese with cottage cheese until smooth. (Or without a food processor, press cottage cheese through a sieve and use a mixer to combine ingredients.) Add sugar, vanilla, cornstarch, eggs, and lemon zest, and process again until smooth. In a bowl, whip cream until soft peaks form and fold into the cheese mixture. Pour into the prepared pan. Bake in the middle of a preheated 325 degree oven for 1 hour. Turn off the oven, leave the oven door ajar, and let cool for 1 hour longer. Chill.

Just before serving, peel and slice kiwi fruit and encircle the top of the cheesecake with the slices. In a small saucepan, heat jelly or honey until runny and drizzle over the fruit. To serve, remove pan sides and cut into wedges.

Makes 12 servings.

Macadamia Nut Crust:

2 teaspoons butter

¼ cup fine graham cracker crumbs (about 4 crackers)

¼ cup macadamia nuts

1 pound natural or regular cream cheese

1 cup large curd cottage cheese

1 cup sugar

2 teaspoons vanilla extract

1 tablespoon cornstarch

4 eggs

1½ teaspoons grated lemon zest

¾ cup heavy cream

2 kiwi fruit

2 tablespoons apricot jelly or honey

Gingered Sweet Potato Cheesecake

This spicy cheesecake with its tantalizing hot sugary ginger topping is a must for the Thanksgiving holiday. Instead of opening a can of pumpkin, it is easy to use a leftover baked sweet potato or yam or to microwave one.

To prepare Ginger Graham Cracker Crust, mix together in a bowl the cracker crumbs, butter, sugar, and ginger. Pat into the bottom and partly up the sides of a greased 9-inch springform pan. Bake in a preheated 325 degree oven for 8 minutes. Let cool.

To prepare filling: Place in a food processor or mixer the cheese and sugar, and process or beat until smooth. Mix in sweet potatoes and eggs. Add cream, vanilla, cinnamon, ginger, and cloves, mixing until smooth. Pour into the crust-lined pan. Bake in the middle of a preheated 325 degree oven for 25 minutes or until just barely set. Turn off the oven, leave door ajar, and let cool in the oven for 1 hour longer. Chill. To serve, sprinkle the top with candied ginger, remove pan sides, and cut in wedges.

Makes 10 servings.

NOTE: To microwave 1 large sweet potato or yam, prick it with a fork in several places, place it on a microwavable dish, and microwave on high for 6 to 8 minutes or until soft. Let cool.

Ginger Graham Cracker Crust:

1 cup crushed graham cracker crumbs

3 tablespoons melted butter

2 tablespoons sugar

½ teaspoon ground ginger

1 pound natural or regular cream cheese

¾ cup firmly packed brown sugar

1¼ cups cooked sweet potatoes, yams, or pumpkin

3 eggs

½ cup heavy cream

1 teaspoon vanilla extract

1 teaspoon ground cinnamon

½ teaspoon ground ginger

¼ teaspoon ground cloves

⅓ cup chopped candied ginger

Golden Apple Cheesecake

Sugar-glazed apple rings top this cognac-laced cheesecake.

Prepare Cinnamon Zweiback Crust: Toss crumbs with butter and cinnamon and press into the bottom and partly up the sides of a 9-inch springform pan. Bake in a preheated 325 degree oven for 8 minutes or until golden brown. Let cool.

Peel, core, and slice apples into ½-inch thick rings. In a large skillet, melt butter and 2 tablespoons sugar over medium-low heat. Add apple rings and saute until soft, turning once to cook through, allowing about 10 minutes. In a food processor or mixer, place the cheese and remaining sugar and process or mix until smooth. Mix in eggs, vanilla, cognac, lemon zest, and sour cream. Reserve 8 apple rings for topping. Arrange remaining apple rings in the bottom of the crust-lined pan. Pour in the cheese filling, smooth top, and arrange reserved apple rings on top. Bake in the middle of a preheated 325 degree oven for 25 minutes or until just barely set. Turn off the oven, leave the door ajar, and let cool in the oven for 1 hour longer. Chill. To serve, remove pan sides and cut into wedges.

Makes 10 servings.

Cinnamon Zweiback Crust:

1¼ cups crushed zweiback crumbs

3 tablespoons butter, melted

½ teaspoon ground cinnamon

5 large tart apples

2 tablespoons butter

¾ cup plus 2 tablespoons sugar

1 pound natural, regular, or Neufchâtel cream cheese

3 eggs

1 teaspoon vanilla extract

2 tablespoons cognac or brandy

1 teaspoon grated lemon zest

¾ cup sour cream

Light-Style Cheesecakes

Frozen Framboise Cheesecakes 48

Candied Ginger Ricotta Cheesecakes 50

Rum Mousse Cheesecake 51

Hawaiian Pineapple Coconut Cheesecake 53

Soufflé Cheesecake with Nectarines 54

Berry-Crowned Yogurt Cheesecake 55

Apricot Pistachio Cheesecake 56

Frozen Framboise Cheesecakes

A goblet of fromage glacé avec framboise *was a dining sensation at a Provençal two-star restaurant years ago. In a lighter adaptation of this theme, yogurt cheese scented with framboise liqueur makes inviting individual dessert molds. This cheese is easily made at home by draining yogurt through a commercial fine-meshed sieve or cheesecloth-lined sieve.*

In a small saucepan, combine the sugar, water, and corn syrup. Bring to a boil and cook until the temperature reaches 238 degrees on a candy thermometer (soft-ball stage). Meanwhile, in an electric mixer, beat egg whites until soft peaks form, then gradually beat in the hot syrup; continue beating at high speed until mixture cools to room temperature, about 7 minutes. In a bowl, whip cream until stiff peaks form and beat in framboise liqueur. Fold in yogurt cheese and egg white meringue. Spoon into individual soufflé dishes, 4 ounces each. Cover and freeze until firm.

½ cup sugar

¼ cup water

1 teaspoon light corn syrup

2 egg whites

½ cup heavy cream

¼ cup framboise liqueur or eau de vie

¾ cup yogurt cheese: see page 49

2 cups raspberries for garnish

Serve in the soufflé dishes or if desired, unmold by dipping each souffle dish in a pan of hot water, release the sides with a sharp knife, and invert mold on a dessert plate. Garnish the top with raspberries.

Makes 6 servings.

YOGURT CHEESE. To make yogurt cheese, use a commercial fine-meshed sieve for cheesemaking or line a sieve with cheesecloth; place it in a bowl to catch the whey as it drains away. Spoon 1 pint unflavored yogurt (made without gelatin) into the sieve. Cover and refrigerate for 12 to 16 hours. The water or whey, about half the amount of yogurt, will drain off, leaving yogurt cheese with a thick consistency comparable to whipped cream cheese. Discard the whey or use it for another purpose, such as in baking yeast breads.

Candied Ginger Ricotta Cheesecakes

Nuggets of candied ginger fleck this orange-scented cheesecake that bakes in individual servings. Take your pick of cheeses—ricotta lends a slightly grainy texture, cottage cheese less so, while yogurt cheese makes it silky smooth.

In a small bowl, mash orange zest with 1 teaspoon of the sugar using the back of a spoon to release oils. Place in the bowl of a food processor or blender the cheese, yogurt, remaining sugar, and eggs, and blend until smooth. Stir in orange zest and 3 tablespoons of the ginger. Pour into lightly greased individual soufflé dishes, 4 ounces in size. Place soufflé dishes in a water bath, a pan with hot water coming halfway up the sides of the dishes. Bake in the middle of a preheated 325 degree oven for 15 to 20 minutes or until cheesecake is set. Remove dishes from the water bath. Let cool on a rack, then chill.

To serve, sprinkle with remaining ginger and place the grapes alongside.

Makes 4 servings.

2 tablespoons finely chopped orange zest

¼ cup sugar

½ pint (8 ounces) large curd cottage cheese, ricotta, or yogurt cheese: see page 49

½ cup low-fat plain yogurt

2 eggs

¼ cup chopped candied ginger

Fresh fruit accompaniment: bunches of green or red seedless grapes

Rum Mousse Cheesecake

A delicate aftertaste of rum infuses this silky smooth cheese creation.

Prepare Cinnamon Graham Cracker Crust: In a small bowl, mix together the cracker crumbs, butter, and cinnamon. Pat into the bottom and ½ inch up the sides of an 8 or 9-inch springform pan. Bake in the middle of a preheated 325 degree oven for 8 minutes. Let cool.

In the top of a double boiler, stir together the sugar, gelatin, and milk. Stir in beaten eggs. Cook over hot water, stirring, until custard coats a spoon. Remove from heat and stir in rum. Place in a pan of ice water to cool. In a food processor or blender, process cheese until smooth. Blend in the cool custard mixture. In a bowl, whip cream until soft peaks form and fold into the cheese custard. Pour into the crust-lined pan and smooth the top. Chill for 2 hours or until set.

To serve, sprinkle with nuts, remove pan sides, and cut into wedges.

Makes 8 to 10 servings.

Cinnamon Graham Cracker Crust:

1 cup crushed graham crackers

2 tablespoons butter, melted

½ teaspoon ground cinnamon

½ cup sugar

1 envelope unflavored gelatin

½ cup milk

2 eggs, lightly beaten

2 tablespoons rum or Amaretto

1½ cups large curd cottage cheese

½ cup heavy cream

3 tablespoons toasted sliced almonds for garnish

Hawaiian Pineapple Coconut Cheesecake

Toasted coconut, pineapple chunks, and sweet macadamia nuts bring a tropical flair to cheesecake patterned in the light style.

Prepare Coconut Crust: Toss coconut with butter and press into the bottom of a 9-inch springform pan. Bake in the middle of a preheated 325 degree oven for 8 to 10 minutes or until golden brown. Let cool.

Place in a food processor or mixer the cheese and sugar, and process or beat until smooth. Mix in eggs, sour cream, and vanilla. Stir in pineapple and turn into the baked crust. Bake in the middle of a preheated 325 degree oven for 25 minutes or until just barely set.

Prepare Sour Cream Topping: In a small bowl, mix together the sour cream or yogurt, sugar, and vanilla and immediately spread over the top of the warm cheesecake. Return to a preheated 350 degree oven and continue baking 5 minutes longer. Turn off the oven, leave the door ajar, and let cool in the oven for 1 hour longer. Chill. At serving time, sprinkle with nuts or coconut. Remove pan sides and cut into wedges.

Makes 8 to 10 servings.

Coconut Crust:

1½ cups coconut flakes

1 tablespoon butter, melted

1 pound Neufchâtel cream cheese

¾ cup sugar

3 eggs

½ cup low-fat sour cream

1 teaspoon vanilla extract

1 cup crushed pineapple or finely diced fresh pineapple

Sour Cream Topping:

¾ cup low-fat sour cream or plain low-fat yogurt

1 tablespoon sugar

½ teaspoon vanilla

⅓ cup chopped macadamia nuts or toasted coconut

Soufflé Cheesecake with Nectarines

With yogurt cheese on hand, this light-style cheesecake whips up in a jiffy, making an ethereal dessert, sized for an intimate dinner.

Lightly butter the bottom and partly up the sides of a 7-inch springform pan or spray it with non-stick spray. Sprinkle with graham cracker crumbs. In a bowl, beat egg whites until soft peaks form and beat in ¼ cup of the sugar, beating until meringue holds stiff upright peaks. In another bowl mix together yogurt cheese, eggs yolks, remaining sugar, and vanilla. Fold in the meringue. Pour into the crumb-lined pan. Bake in the middle of a pre-heated 325 degree oven for 20 minutes or until risen and golden brown on the edges. Turn off the oven, leave the oven door ajar, and let cool in the oven for 15 minutes.

Serve warm or at room temperature. Remove pan sides, cut into wedges, and accompany with fruit spooned alongside.

Makes 4 servings.

½ teaspoon butter or non-stick spray

1 tablespoon fine graham cracker crumbs

2 eggs, separated

¼ cup plus 1½ table-spoons sugar

¾ cup yogurt cheese: see page 49

1½ teaspoons vanilla extract

2 nectarines, halved, pitted, and sliced, or 1 cup blackberries or raspberries or a combination of fruit for garnish

Berry-Crowned Yogurt Cheesecake

A refreshing duo of berries cloaks this light-style cheesecake for a party-pleaser trimmed of fat.

Lightly butter the bottom and partly up the sides of a 7-inch springform pan or spray it with non-stick spray. Sprinkle with cracker crumbs. In a bowl, beat eggs until light in color and beat in sugar, vanilla, and Amaretto, beating until light and frothy. Mix in yogurt cheese and yogurt. Pour into the crumb-lined pan. Bake in the middle of a 325 degree oven for 20 minutes or until just barely set. Let cool on a rack, then chill.

Halve strawberries, if large, and lightly mix with raspberries and sugar to taste. To serve, remove pan sides, top with berries, and cut into wedges.

Makes 4 servings.

½ teaspoon butter or non-stick spray

1½ tablespoons fine graham cracker crumbs

2 eggs

⅓ cup sugar

1 teaspoon vanilla extract

1 tablespoon Amaretto

1 cup yogurt cheese: see page 49

½ cup low-fat plain yogurt

1½ cups mixed berries: strawberries and raspberries or blueberries or blackberries

Sugar to taste

Apricot Pistachio Cheesecake

This snowy white soufflé cheesecake is punctuated with tangy dried apricots and a crunchy pistachio praline topping.

Place apricots in a microwavable bowl, sprinkle with 2 tablespoons of the liqueur, and microwave for 2 minutes or until hot through. Or bake in a preheated 325 degree oven for 10 minutes or until hot. Let cool. Place in a food processor or blender the cottage cheese, cream cheese, vanilla, and remaining 2 tablespoons liqueur and process until smooth. In a large bowl, beat egg whites until soft peaks form and gradually beat in the sugar, beating until stiff but not dry. Fold one-third of the whites into the cheese mixture to lighten it; then fold cheese mixture and apricots into the remaining egg whites. Pour into a greased 9-inch springform pan. Bake in the middle of a preheated 350 degree oven for 25 minutes or until just barely set.

½ cup dried apricots, finely chopped

4 tablespoons orange-flavored liqueur

1 pint low-fat cottage cheese

1 package (8 ounces) Neufchâtel cream cheese

1 teaspoon vanilla extract

4 egg whites

¾ cup sugar

Yogurt Topping:

¾ cup low-fat plain yogurt

1 tablespoon sugar

1 teaspoon vanilla extract

Pistachio Praline:

1 teaspoon butter

1 tablespoon sugar

¼ cup chopped roasted pistachios

Prepare Yogurt Topping: Mix together yogurt, sugar, and vanilla, and immediately spread over the top of the warm cheesecake. Return to a 350 degree oven and bake 5 minutes longer or until set. Turn off the oven, leave the door ajar, and let cool in the oven for 1 hour longer. Chill.

Prepare Pistachio Praline: In a small skillet heat butter and sugar over medium heat, add pistachios and heat until nuts are lightly toasted and glazed with caramel coating, shaking pan constantly. Turn out onto waxed paper and let cool. To serve, sprinkle Pistachio Praline over cheesecake. Remove pan sides and cut into wedges.

Makes 10 servings.

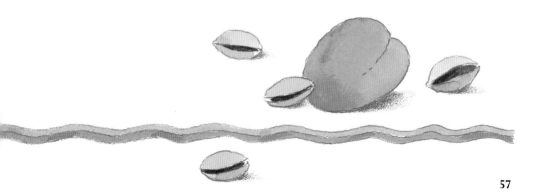

Savory Cheesecakes

Smoked Salmon Cheesecake 60

Pesto Pistachio Cheese Torte 62

Filo-Wrapped Havarti Cheesecake 63

Santa Fe Cheesecake 64

Camembert with Mushroom Melange 66

Brie Round Provençal 67

Cheese and Mushroom Borek 68

Smoked Salmon Cheesecake

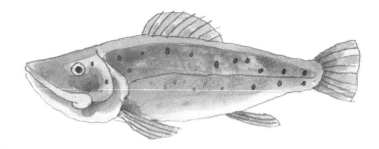

This light-style savory appetizer makes an impressive first course or luncheon entrée. Another time, vary the topping with small cooked shrimp.

Prepare Rye Crust: In a blender or food processor, grind crackers until fine. Add butter and pulse to mix. Press into the bottom of a 9-inch springform pan. Bake in a preheated 325 degree oven for 8 minutes. Let cool.

In a food processor or mixer, process or beat the cream cheese until creamy and mix in the eggs, sour cream, Jarlsberg cheese, parsley, chives, tarragon, and pepper. Pour into the crust-lined pan. Bake in the middle of a preheated 325 degree oven for 20 minutes or until just barely set. Turn off the oven, leave the door ajar, and let cool in the oven for 1 hour longer. Chill.

Rye Crust:

12 Rye Krisp crackers

2 tablespoons melted butter or olive oil

2 packages (8 ounces each) Neufchâtel cream cheese

2 eggs

⅓ cup low-fat sour cream

½ cup shredded light Jarlsberg cheese

2 tablespoons chopped fresh flat-leaf parsley

2 tablespoons chopped
fresh chives

1 teaspoon crumbled
dried tarragon

¼ teaspoon freshly
ground black pepper

Flat-leaf parsley sprigs
for garnish

6 ounces smoked salmon

2 tablespoons capers

2 green onions, chopped

Just before serving, place parsley sprigs around the edge. Cut salmon into 1-inch strips and arrange in a ring on the top of the filling. Scatter capers over the top. Sprinkle onions in a ring inside the salmon. Remove pan sides and cut into wedges.

Makes 10 to 12 servings.

Pesto Pistachio Cheese Torte

Ribbons of pesto stripe this creamy white cheesecake for a taste-tingling spread on toasted baguette slices. Shaped in a round charlotte mold or even a clean flower pot, the decorative cheese makes a stunning presentation on a party table.

Prepare Pesto: In a food processor or blender, place the basil, spinach, parsley, garlic, and pistachios. Process until finely minced. Add oil and blend for 1 minute to incorporate. Blend in Parmesan cheese. Remove from container and set aside.

In a food processor or mixer, blend the cheeses until combined. Line a 6-inch charlotte mold or cylindrical mold with a double layer of dampened cheesecloth. Spoon in one-third of the cheese mixture and spread in an even layer. Cover with half of the Pesto, spreading evenly. Repeat, using one-third of the cheese mixture and remaining Pesto. Top with remaining cheese and spread evenly. Cover and chill for 2 hours or longer to firm up.

To serve, unmold and place on a serving platter. Surround with toasted baguette slices or crackers. Place a cheese knife alongside so guests may cut the mold into wedges.

Makes 12 servings.

Pesto:

1 cup firmly packed fresh basil leaves

1 cup firmly packed spinach leaves

½ cup firmly packed fresh flat-leaf parsley leaves

3 cloves garlic, minced

3 tablespoons pistachios, minced

¼ cup olive oil

½ cup grated Parmesan cheese

1 pound natural or regular cream cheese

¼ pound Gorgonzola or other blue cheese

Toasted baguette slices or stone-ground crackers

Filo-Wrapped Havarti Cheesecake

Crispy layers of filo make a handsome pouf encasing Havarti cheese strewn with pistachios and fresh rosemary. When cut, the creamy cheese oozes to an unctuous spread that's scrumptious with fruit.

Stack filo sheets on a board and trim one end to create a 13-inch square. (Use the cut-off strip for another purpose.) Lay 1 sheet on the work surface and cover the others with plastic wrap. Brush the filo sheet with butter and sprinkle with one-third of the crumbs. Place a second sheet on top of the first and repeat the process. Repeat with the third sheet and remaining crumbs. Top with the fourth sheet, butter it, and place the cheese in the middle of the stacked filo. Sprinkle with rosemary and nuts. Bring the four corners of the filo square together and twist securely to enclose the cheese. Spread out the ends to form a pouf. Brush filo with remaining butter. Place on a buttered baking sheet. If desired, assemble 2 to 3 hours in advance, cover with plastic wrap, and refrigerate. Uncover, bake in the middle of a preheated 350 degree oven until the filo is golden brown, about 18 to 20 minutes. Remove from the oven and let cool a few minutes. Transfer to a serving platter.

Halve, core, and slice pears or apples and encircle the cheese. Let guests savor a wedge of pastry-wrapped cheese and fruit, served on small plates with forks.

Makes 6 to 8 servings.

4 sheets filo pastry (approximately 13 by 17 inches), thawed

3 tablespoons butter, melted

¼ cup dry white bread crumbs or brioche

7 ounce round creamy Havarti cheese

1 tablespoon fresh rosemary, chopped

3 tablespoons chopped pistachios or pine nuts

3 pears or apples

NOTE: *If a round of creamy Havarti is unavailable, select a square of Havarti or Samsoe cheese, cut about 1 inch high and 4 inches across.*

Santa Fe Cheesecake

With a Southwestern pizzazz, a fresh fruit salsa punctuates this chili-spiced cheesecake. Fill a basket with blue corn chips for scoopers for both.

Prepare Corn Chip Crust: In a bowl, toss together the corn chips and oil or butter. Pat into the bottom and partly up the sides of a greased 9-inch pie pan. Bake in a preheated 325 degree oven for 6 minutes.

In a small skillet, heat oil and sauté shallots until soft. Add garlic and sauté for 1 minute. In a food processor or mixer, place cream cheese and process until blended. Add eggs and blend until smooth. Mix in cream, chili powder, cumin, oregano, parsley, and sauteed shallots. Season with salt and pepper to taste. Pour into the crust-lined pan and sprinkle seeds over the top. Bake in the middle of a preheated 325 degree oven for 20 minutes or until just barely set. Turn off the oven, leave oven door ajar, and let cool in the oven for 1 hour longer. Chill.

Corn Chip Crust:

¾ cup crushed corn chips or blue corn chips

1 tablespoon olive oil or butter, melted

1 teaspoon olive oil

¼ cup minced shallots or sweet onions

1 clove garlic, minced

12 ounces natural or regular cream cheese

2 eggs

¼ cup heavy cream

½ teaspoon chili powder

½ teaspoon ground cumin

½ teaspoon crumbled dried oregano or 2 teaspoons fresh oregano

2 tablespoons minced fresh flat-leaf parsley

Salt and freshly ground pepper to taste

¼ cup sunflower seeds

Fruit Salsa:

3 nectarines, peeled, pitted, and diced, or 3 firm, ripe tomatoes, peeled, seeded, and chopped

1 small sweet red or white onion, finely chopped

1 small green chili pepper, seeded and chopped, or 2 to 3 tablespoons chopped canned green chili peppers

Salt and pepper to taste

½ teaspoon sugar

2 tablespoons cilantro, chopped

Corn chips or blue corn chips

Prepare Fruit Salsa: Mix together in a bowl the nectarines or tomatoes, onions, chili peppers, salt, pepper, sugar, and cilantro. Cover and chill for 1 hour for flavors to blend. Makes about 3 cups.

To serve, remove pan sides and cut into wedges. Accompany with a bowl of Fruit Salsa and a basket of corn chips.

Makes 8 servings.

Camembert with Mushroom Melange

The fresh aroma of herbs and mushrooms swaths a disc of warmly runny Camembert.

In a skillet over medium-high heat, sauté shallots in oil until soft. Add the garlic and sauté 1 minute longer, stirring. Add the mushrooms and cook for 1 minute. Remove from heat and stir in herbs and nuts. Place Camembert on a sheet of foil on a baking sheet. Spread the cooked mushroom mixture on top of the cheese. If desired, refrigerate for up to 4 hours before baking. Shortly before serving, arrange the slices of bread on a baking sheet and bake in a preheated 350 degree oven until lightly toasted, about 5 minutes. Keep warm. Bake the cheese in the middle of a preheated 350 degree oven for 6 to 8 minutes or just until warm through. Carefully transfer the Camembert on the foil to a serving platter and trim away excess foil. Or serve the cheese at room temperature and top with the warm mushroom mixture.

Serve surrounded with the toasted bread and garnish with basil sprigs. Place a cheese knife alongside for guests to use.

Makes 8 servings.

1 tablespoon olive oil

3 shallots, finely chopped

2 cloves garlic, minced

½ pound button mushrooms, sliced

2 tablespoons chopped fresh herbs: a mixture of basil, oregano, and parsley

2 tablespoons chopped pistachios or pine nuts

8-ounce round of Camembert or Brie

1 baguette, sliced ½ inch thick

Basil sprigs for garnish

Brie Round Provençal

Sealing over a warm cake of Brie is a cloak of Provençal flavors —sun-dried tomatoes, Niçoise olives, sweet onions, basil, and pistachios. The aromatic melange is a zestful partner with the softly oozing cheese, spread on crispy baguette slices.

In a skillet over medium-high heat, heat the oil and sauté onions until soft. Add the garlic and sauté 1 minute longer, stirring. Add the tomatoes and basil and cook for 1 minute. Remove from heat and stir in olives and nuts. Place Brie on a sheet of foil on a baking sheet. Spread the cooked sun-dried tomato mixture on top of the cheese. If desired, refrigerate for up to 4 hours before baking. Shortly before serving, arrange the slices of bread on a baking sheet and bake in a preheated 350 degree oven until lightly toasted, about 5 minutes. Keep warm. Bake the cheese in the middle of a preheated 350 degree oven for 6 to 8 minutes or just until warm through. Carefully transfer the Brie on the foil to a serving platter and trim away excess foil. Or serve the Brie at room temperature and top with the warm sun-dried tomato mixture.

Serve surrounded with the toasted bread and garnish with basil sprigs. Place a cheese knife alongside for guests to use.

Makes 8 servings.

1 tablespoon olive oil

1 small sweet onion, finely chopped

2 cloves garlic, minced

12 sun-dried tomatoes, packed in oil or otherwise flexible

2 tablespoons chopped fresh basil

¼ cup pitted Niçoise olives, chopped

2 tablespoons chopped pistachios or pine nuts

8-ounce round of Brie

1 baguette, sliced ½ inch thick

Basil sprigs for garnish

Cheese and Mushroom Borek

Flaky crisp layers of filo encase the softly melting quartet of cheeses in this savory mushroom pie. Cut it in squares for an appetizer or in wedges for a first course offering.

Lay out pastry on a board, cover with plastic wrap, and let warm to room temperature. In a skillet heat oil and sauté onions until soft. Add mushrooms and sauté for 1 minute; turn out of the pan into a bowl and let cool. In a food processor, place the cream cheese, cottage cheese, feta, Jarlsberg cheese, egg, parsley, and pepper, and process until blended.

Lightly butter a 10-inch springform pan and lay 1 sheet of filo in the bottom of the pan, letting it drape over the sides. With a pastry brush, lightly butter filo and sprinkle with one-third of the crumbs. Cover with another sheet of filo so the corners overlap another part of the pan. Lightly butter filo and sprinkle with another third of the crumbs. Repeat with a third sheet of filo, lightly butter it, and sprinkle with remaining crumbs. Cover with a fourth sheet of filo. Pour filling into the filo-lined pan, spreading it smooth. Cover with sauteed mushrooms.

Cut the remaining 2 sheets of filo in half. Place one sheet on top of mushrooms and fold down the overlapping corners of filo. Lightly butter filo and lay the remaining

6 sheets filo pastry (approximately 13 by 17 inches), thawed

1 tablespoon olive oil

¼ cup chopped sweet onion or shallots

¼ pound mushrooms, sliced

4 ounces regular or natural cream cheese

8 ounces (1 cup) large curd cottage cheese

4 ounces feta cheese, crumbled

4 ounces light Jarlsberg cheese, shredded

1 egg

¼ cup chopped fresh parsley

Freshly ground black pepper to taste

2 to 3 tablespoons butter, melted

½ cup fine bread crumbs

sheets of filo on top, tucking under the corners and but-
tering each sheet. If desired, cover lightly with plastic
wrap and refrigerate for up to 2 hours before baking.

Bake in the middle of a preheated 375 degree oven for
20 to 22 minutes or until golden brown. Let cool on a
rack for at least 15 minutes or up to 1 hour, to firm up.
Remove pan sides and cut into wedges or squares.

Makes 8 to 10 first course servings or 30 appetizer squares.

Index

Table of Equivalents

The exact equivalents in the following tables have been rounded for convenience.

Weights			Liquids			Length Measures	
US/UK	Metric	US	Metric	UK		US/UK	Metric
1 oz	30 g	2 tbl	30 ml	1 fl oz		⅛ in	3 mm
2 oz	60 g	¼ cup	60 ml	2 fl oz		¼ in	6 mm
3 oz	90 g	⅓ cup	80 ml	3 fl oz		½ in	12 mm
4 oz (¼ lb)	125 g	½ cup	125 ml	4 fl oz		1 in	2.5 cm
5 oz (⅓ lb)	155 g	⅔ cup	160 ml	5 fl oz		2 in	5 cm
6 oz	185 g	¾ cup	180 ml	6 fl oz		3 in	7.5 cm
7 oz	220 g	1 cup	250 ml	8 fl oz		4 in	10 cm
8 oz (½ lb)	250 g	1½ cups	375 ml	12 fl oz		5 in	13 cm
10 oz	315 g	2 cups	500 ml	16 fl oz		6 in	15 cm
12 oz (¾ lb)	375 g	4 c/1 qt	1 liter	32 fl oz		7 in	18 cm
14 oz	440 g					8 in	20 cm
16 oz (1 lb)	500 g					9 in	23 cm
1½ lbs	750 g					10 in	25 cm
2 lbs	1 kg					11 in	28 cm
3 lbs	1.5 kg					12 in/1 ft	30 cm

Oven Temperatures

Fahrenheit	Celsius	Gas
250	120	½
275	140	1
300	150	2
325	160	3
350	180	4
375	190	5
400	200	6
425	220	7
450	230	8
475	240	9
500	260	10